To Laurel &
Ethan

See you @ the Movies

Jon Bonton
11/2/15

Movies in a Minute

The Essence of the 100 Greatest Films
Distilled into a Page or Two of Poetry

TOM PONTAC

authorHOUSE®

AuthorHouse™
1663 Liberty Drive
Bloomington, IN 47403
www.authorhouse.com
Phone: 1-800-839-8640

Tom Pontac/Poetic License

Published by AuthorHouse 10/25/2014

ISBN: 978-1-4969-4779-6 (sc)
ISBN: 978-1-4969-4780-2 (e)

Library of Congress Control Number: 2014918707

"Mr. Pontac is an Astonishingly Cleaver Versifier whose short, terse and witty lines capture the plot essence of everybody's favorite movie."

Steve Allen, comedian, author and songwriter

"Tom Pontac was a Surprise I never expected. He definitely has The Gift. Where did he come from?"

Marshall Baher, lyricist, songwriter,
composer of "Once Upon A Mattress"

DEDICATED TO ALL WHO HAVE BEEN TOUCHED
BY THE STORIES AND IMAGES OF THE MOVIES AND
NEED ONLY A JOYFUL HINT OF THEIR ESSENCE TO
'PLAY THEM AGAIN' ON THE FLICKERING SCREENS
OF OUR MINDS, IMAGINATIONS AND MEMORIES..

WITHIN THE DARK,
UPON THE SCREEN
IS OUR
IMAGINATION SEEN
THE FUTURE'S TIMES
AND AGES PAST,
FORBIDDEN LOVES,
AN ENDLESS CAST
OF HEROS, COWARDS,
DREAMS AND DUST,
OF SAINTS AND SINNERS
VIRTUE, LUST,
OF SONGS AND LIGHTS,
OF WRONGS AND RIGHTS,
OF LIES REVEALED,
OF LOVE'S DELIGHTS
WE OFFER YOU
THIS PANOPLY:
100 YEARS OF
HISTORY
100 POEMS
TO HELP YOU FIND
YOUR FAVORITE MOVIES,
IN YOUR MIND.....

TO MY WIFE, JEANNE, WITH LOVE, FOR ALL
HER LOVE AND ENCOURAGEMENT, AND
JAN MARSHALL, LOVING FRIEND, WHO
ALWAYS BELIEVED I COULD DO IT!

Contents

1. Citizen Kane

A giant gate
A foggy dew
Reveals the
Castle Xanadu
A lighted pane,
A lonely room,
Displayed within
This shuttered gloom,
A dying man,
A single word,
"Rosebud,"
Nothing more is heard
A lifeless hand
Lets loose to fall
A storm imprisoned
In a ball
Charles Foster Kane,
As all men must,
Saw life and fortune
Turn to dust
Men pondered what
His last word meant
Unknowing that
His life was spent

In a desperate search to find

That peaceful world

He'd left behind

Kane's fortune robbed

His life of love

Now smoke and ashes

Curl above

The shuttered hulk

Of Xanadu

Where sled and

Innocence

Pass through

How brief is life

This story tells-

A masterpiece

By Orson Wells

2. Casablanca

French Morocco,'41
War has Europe
On the run
Everybody
Stops to stay
For a while at Rick's Café
It's Bogart, Bergman
And a story
Filled with romance,
Honor, glory
(Plus Claude Rains
And Peter Lorre)
Sam plays again
"As Time Goes By"
Shows Fundamental
Things Apply
As Rick remembers
What they did,
When he said,
"Looking at you, kid"
As time went by
War tore apart
All but the love
Within their heart

Again Rick lets her go
And fly
To safety though
The darkening sky
And knows the sacrifice
He did,
Looks up, says,
"Looking at you, kid."
Shoots German as
Gendarmes arrive,
So love and honor
Can survive
"The usual suspects,"
French cop states,
Just, "Round them up!"
And seals their fates
The fog rolls in,
The world keeps spinning
'A beautiful friendship'
Is beginning!

3. The Godfather

Here's the good
And awful news
His offer's one
You can't refuse
The Don is one,
You do his wishes
Unless you want
To sleep with fishes
The Great American
Dream come true
Written in blood red,
White and blue
He pulls the strings
Hits happen and
All done with a
Fine Italian hand
He's the "Local
Italian boy makes good"
And the head of the
'Family' Neighborhood

4. Gone With The Wind

Ante Bellum,

Southern Belle

Civil War turns

South to Hell

Rhett and Scarlet,

Rogue and Lady

Share a romance

Fast and Shady

While Devastation

Grips the nation

Scarlet holds tight

To plantation

We can see

Atlanta Burning

As we see

Our Scarlet Yearning

For a love that's

Most forbidden

Scarlet keeps her

Passions hidden

Post war peace,

Means Reconstruction

From the Civil War's

Destruction

Rhett really tries
To let her know
That he's the one
Who loves her so
He offers love
So she'll believe
She spurns, he turns,
And goes to leave
Too late, she knows
"I love this man!"
But, frankly, he
"Don't give a damn!"
Oh well, says she,
I always say,
"Tomorrow is another day!"

5. Lawrence Of Arabia

Englishman,
Dressed all in white,
Shows desert Bedouins
How to fight
Desert Bedouin,
Dressed in black,
Helps white faced
Englishman attack
They blow up trains
And ride the sand
An Anti-Turkish
Traveling Band
And serve both
Bedouin and king,
Who think this Englishman's
The thing,
Invincible and
Super strong
Turks capture him
And prove them wrong
They break his body,
Not his will,
He, still,
Has destiny to fill

"Lead one more time?"
They plead
"Just ask us!"
He replies,
"On to Damascus!"
With Arab victory,
Total, whole,
Lawrence loses
English soul
Back in England,
Freed from strife,
Lawrence loses
English life

6. The Wizard Of Oz

Kansas Wind comes up, non-soto
Lifts Dorothy, house and dog-en Toto!
Whirls All up, then Swirls it down
Witch is squished in Munchkin Town
Witch's Sister threatens Dot
Hot for Ruby shoes she's got
On to Oz, Old Wizard there
Will wash the witch from Dorothy's hair
Stout Companions, Scarecrow, Tin
Man and the Lion finally win
An Audience with Noble Wiz
Who'll gift them if they'll do His Biz
To wit: Bring broomstick back from foe
So to her castle they all go
Through forest, fights and helter skelter
They succeed and finally melt her!
Wiz exposed! An Old Man he
Gives brains, courage and heart to three
Poor Dorothy thinks she's left behind
Until she clicks her heels to find
She's back in Kansas, what a sight-
The colors gone-She's black and white!

7. The Graduate

Sounds of Silence wrap around
Our hero Ben, who's Homeward Bound
And finds he hasn't got a clue
On what to say, or what to do
Ben sees ahead a plastic life
Now enter fathers' partners' wife!
Ben takes her home,
She takes her hose off!
Ben starts to sweat,
She takes her clothes off!
He wants to leave, she says, "Ben dear,"
"Any time you want, I'm here!"
He goes but, in a day, our Ben
Calls Mrs. Robinson again
This time both have no thought of waiting
Instantly they're conjugating
No single word in bed is said
Sounds of Silence heard, instead
Daughter comes home, younger version
Of Bens' amorous perversion,
He prefers the Miss To Mrs.
Confesses all, as Mother hisses
Both despise him, curse his name

Alone, he sits and writes, "Elaine."
Invades her wedding she's deciding
To elope with Ben, and riding
In a bus, sans Mom and groom,
And 'Graduates' to Honeymoon!

8. On The Waterfront

Instead of anguish,
Never ending,
He could have been,
At least,
Contending
Now on the docks,
And not the ring
He feels his life's
A hollow thing
And realizes,
That the Mob,
Which he despises,
Keeps his job
And to avenge
The ones who died
Would only get him
Crucified!
A Saintly gal
Wins over Terry
He's got to be
The man she'll marry,
His brothers death
Convinces Terry-
To learn to sing

Like a canary,

He's beaten, broken,

But unbowed,

And leads the

Cheering Union Crowd!

So, in it's rough

And tumble way

Truth and courage

Have their day

9. Schindler's List

Hitler's Nazis
Take their toll
Otto Schindler
Finds his soul
In this brutal,
Killing nation
Schindler's List
Gives both
Salvation
Within this harsh
And brutal place
Schindler and his list
Gave grace
His dark
And tortured soul
Made light
And shined a candle
In the night
His life had meaning
So we save
A prayer to honor
Schindler's grave

10. Singin' In The Rain

Reel and real life

Come together

Like sunny days

And rainy weather

When dance and songs

Got integrated

And loves' emotions

Liberated

As people voiced

Their passions strong

As if by chance

In dance and song

This musical's

A brand new game

When silents went

And talkies came

Kelly and O'Connor

Whirl

Across the screen

To get the girl

On back stages

Down the halls

Across our hearts

And up the walls

Kelly's love won't wait
A minute
Not only dancing up a storm-
But in it!
Just like a child
With love's sweet pain
He's swinging,
"Singing in the rain"
Eventually,
Love's truth is seen
As Kelly, Reynolds
Are a team
In love's embrace
We too will find
The rain's sweet songs
Within our mind

11. It's A Wonderful Life

In Bedford Falls, George Bailey's dreams
Have turned to dust, or so it seems
His life's responsibilities and debt
Were obligations, always met
But now, bereft of dreams and hope,
He feels at the end of his rope
The angels look and know they must
Reveal the gold within the dust
For George, with all his dreams thus torn,
Now wishes he had not been born
A novice angel, A.F.C.,
Reveals to him how life would be
And what would happen, how he'd feel
If, in fact, his wish were real
All those not helped, lives not made whole,
Through the goodness of his soul
His presence gone, old hurts unhealed,
George sees life's meaning now revealed
He finds life's wonderful today
Gods gift he cannot throw away!
And we discover, as this ends,
No man's a failure, who has friends
And as his family gathers round,
Know he's the richest man in town.

12. Sunset Boulevard

Body floating

Dead relating

Star emoting

Corpse narrating

Norma's story

Silent glory

Movie queen,

Silver screen

Career crashes

Falls to ashes

Sits for years

Alone in hall

Waits for C.

De Mille to call

One day seeing

Young man fleeing

Gives him refuge

He can't refuse,

First he lays her,

Then betrays her

Exits past her,

She moves faster

Plugs that cruel guy,

(Now the pool guy)

Start's emoting
He? Well, floating!
Final ending
Stairs, descending,
Strong and steady
Norma's ready-
Eyes wide, nose up
Final close up!

13. The Bridge On
The River Kwai

Imprisoned in
A foreign land
British soldiers
Take their stand
Build a bridge
Keep their pride
Give the Japanese
A ride
Here the test
Of wills expresses
As captors, captives
Feel distresses
Duty struggles
With their pride
As each confronts
The others side
The bridge goes up,
But undercover,
The bridge blows up
As we discover
This metaphor of life
They bring:
All tried to do
"The proper thing."

14. Some Like It Hot

Valentine's Day,

Execution

Witnesses need

Fast solution

Musicians find that

Gender bending

Keeps career, and life,

From ending

Curtis/Lemmon have

To shave all

Face and arms and legs

To save all

Escaping with an

All girl band

Is almost more than

They can stand

Marilyn M.

In nightgown posing

Almost tempts them

To exposing

Their desires

And their sexes

Sure to turn their lives

To Ex'es

The frantic action
Keeps you guessing
Star crossed lovers
Are cross dressing
No one's perfect
Love beats lie
As guy gets girl,
And guy gets guy!

15. Star Wars

Long time ago,
And far away
In a Galaxy
They say
The Rebel (Good Guy)
Forces fight
Bad Darth Vader
Black as night
It's a Classic
Story told
With captured princess,
Heroes bold,
Droid companions,
Helping fight
A Warrior wise,
A Jedi Knight,
Future western,
Jet ski horses,
Warping spaceships,
Light swords, Forces
A banged up future-
Great F/X-
Gosh!
Almost everything,

But sex,
Didactic and
Galactic story
Filled with romance,
Fun and glory
As good, triumphant,
Wins the day
We knew that it
Would end this way
But it's not over,
At the end
And waiting for us,
Round the bend,
Are sequels (prequels?)
Making three
To form the
Star Wars Trilogy!

16. All About Eve

Success, no matter

What the cost

Have honor, scruples

Torn and tossed

Fasten seat belts,

For this flight

It's going to be

A bumpy night

Wet-eyed, all innocence

And guile,

Eve worms her winsome way

With style

Enchanting almost all

To see

Her melancholy

History

First Margo

And her friends believe

The shy and lovely

Charm of Eve

But as the story

Will reveal

Her words don't indicate

What's real

This classic masterpiece
Displays
With insight
How ambition plays
With subterfuge
And inner drives
Manipulating
Other's lives
Eve's duplicity and fires
Reward her with
Her heart's desires
But as the story ends
Believe,
What Eve has given,
She'll receive
We all discover,
At what cost,
Exactly what was won,
And lost.............

17. The African Queen

Drinking boatman
Forced to ferry
Thinking, lady
Missionary
Thrown together,
World War I,
Find they have to
Make a run
Down the wild
Uncharted straits,
Jungle river,
And their fates
Both, entwined,
Helps them in seeing
Each other's inner soul,
And being
Defeating dangers,
Conquering fear,
Both say those words
Each longs to hear-
They open up
Each others heart
Then blow the

Enemy apart!
Romance and victory
Are one
They float off
In the setting sun

18. Psycho

Crazy Mother, Crazy Son,
Guess what?
Both of them, are one!
Play a while
This side of Hell?
Stay a while
At Bate's Hotel!
Yearn to earn
A heart attack?
Take a shower-
Watch your back!
Although it's black
And white,
You'll swear
The blood red color's
Really there!
A. Hitchcock gives us
All a fright,
Plus Lesson One-
Stay home at night!

19. Chinatown

Polanski's private eye
Film noir
Leaves hearts
And senses both
In awe
With Nicholson
And Dunaway,
The 1930's,
Old L. A.
Hard boiled P. I.,
Cultured lady,
Share a romance
Dark and shady
Where water, power,
Passions, lust
Turn lives and fortunes
Into dust
A convoluted web
Of lies
That wraps around
The truth and tries
To hide corruption,
Evil, sin
But, in the end,

They finally win
Good struggles in
This film with fate
To give us answers
That we hate
Don't let this movie
Get you down,
"Forget it, Jake.
It's Chinatown!"

20. One Flew
Over The Cuckoo's Nest

Nicholson is
At his best
Feathering his
Cuckoo nest
He rejects a
Prison gig
And selects
The psycho brig
Tries to offer
Sanity
To the
Inhumanity
Practiced by the
Awful Nurse
Who's like a Nazi,
Only worse!
His vain attempts
To bring a breath
Of life into
This ward of death
Has authorities
Downsizing
Jack by forced

Lobotomizing
Now at last
His soul is free
To be what it was
Meant to be
While theirs remains
As bad or worse-
Whose the patient?
Whose the nurse?

21. The Grapes Of Wrath

The Great Depression's heavy load
Presented through the Family Joad
The Dust Bowl, and the endless drought
Has forced the family to move out
To leave behind their old life and
Travel to the 'Promised Land'
As migrants come, in endless streams,
To find the answers to their dreams
They find instead an empty hole
Another Dust Bowl of the soul
Where rich exploit and poor are used
Their souls and bodies both abused
The Family Joad keeps up the fight
To carry on, to do what's right,
Tom's forced to flee but says that he
Will fight injustice and will be
Always there, their land is gone
But, in him, honesty lives on
Ma Joad, though beaten, still will act
Her faith and courage both intact
The family's dignity prevails
Through all life's brutal, harsh travails
And, in the end, that strength's ensuring
The Family Joad will be enduring

22. 2001: A Space Odyssey

An ancient past world,

Harsh and mean

A race of

Not quite men are seen

Into this atmosphere

Foreboding

Appears an Obelisk

Promoting

Evolu-Acceleration

For this Ape-man

Population

The stone is touched

It moves their mind

They turn to leave

Their past behind

Now time and

Evolution move

Along the Temporal-

Spatial groove

Man reaches past

The sky and soon

His footsteps lie

Upon the moon

He finds beneath

The Lunar crust
An obelisk
Within the dust
It leads him to
Another place
Across the black uncharted space
A mighty ship with little men
Sets off upon
The path again
A voice through stellar deeps
Has spoken
Man's not alone,
(Now HAL gets broken)
The final obelisk appears
Revealing man kinds
Hopes and fears,
Who knows what other
Worlds may be
Ahead in mankind's destiny?
(We don't know what to make of it-Just Zarathustra spake of it!)

23. The Maltese Falcon

Foggy Ally

Gunshot rings

Truth, betrayal

Fat Man sings

Covets Black Bird

Made of Gold

Tells a story

Quaint and Old

Asks Sam Spade

To dig around

And unearth Bird

From Histories Ground

Sam does deed but finds,

Hot Damn!

Fat Man, girlfriend, Bird

Are Sham!

Trust, Love, Honor,

All are dead

Like the Bird-

Not gold but lead!

Nothing's ever

What it seems

In our hands,

The stuff of dreams…

24. Raging Bull

Rage and torment's
Passion bring
Jake La Motta
To the ring
Private demons
Fill him full
Of pain that wraps
Around his soul
Locked into
His angry cage
With bars of
Bitterness and rage
This tortured fighter
Tears apart
His life, his marriage
And his heart
Every contest,
Every fight,
Is fought in brutal
Black and white
Every foe he fights,
To win,
Except his enemies

Within
Those inner demons
Bring him down
And turn the king
Into the clown

25. E.T.-The Extraterrestrial

From another world,

E. T.,

And Spielberg

Weave their fantasy

Of childhoods innocence

And glory

Into a new

An ageless story

With innocence

And lost souls meeting

Exchanging Universal

Greeting

Of 'calling home'

And finding where

Their homes might lie-

Inside? Out there?

E.T.'s heart light soon

Reveals

Those truths that love

And friendship feels

Both sail across the moon

And find

The worlds they thought

They'd left behind

Though far apart
Both always know
Within their hearts,
Each others glow
Both parable and allegory
This Lucus Light
And Magic Story

26. Dr. Strangelove Or: How I Learned To Stopped Worrying And Love The Bomb

Kubrick's Comedy
Satire's
The Cold Wars nuclear
Bomb desires
Apocalyptic vision of
Earth's final war
And those who love
To play this fearful-
Nightmare game
The Worlds Destruction,
In its name
Peter Sellers
Tour de forces
Has him riding
All three horses
As President,
He has to choose,
As Group Captain,
He's bound to lose,
As Dr. Strangelove
He's psychotic

With a touch
Of Hun, despotic,
Erotic symbols
As selected
Seeing sex and war,
Connected,
Major Kong,
With legs a striding
A-bomb down
Which he is riding,
Confirms mankind's
Most awful fears-
But only for
A hundred years!
Don't worry,
You know what they say,
"Well meet again
Some sunny day..."

27. Bonnie And Clyde

Rural Texas,

1930,

Waitress feeling

Hot and dirty

Enter robber,

Clyde by name,

Offers Bonnie

Bandit fame

Bonnie fondles

Clydes big gun

Helps him pull a heist

And run

Needs adventure,

Has her fill,

As Bonnie learns

To rob and kill

They take money

Tell folks, "Thanks,

We're Bonnie and Clyde

And we rob banks!"

Then speed away

With banjos playing,

Cops and robbers,

Bullets spraying,

In the end,
They end up dying
As they're trying
For their glory-
End of story

28. Apocalypse Now

Francis Coppola
Describes
The sensual madness
Battle hides
And shows within
Our darkest heart
There lies a mad,
Immoral part
The words of
Martin Sheen reveal
The madness that war
Makes men feel
The horror that is
Justified
As hopes and morals
Are denied
Napalms smell
Invades like breath
And pervades this
World of death
Sheens orders are
'To terminate
With prejudice',
A man whose fate

Was to accept insanity
At cost of his
Humanity
And dark within
His heart to be
What others could
Or would not see
Brando,
Soul and body worn,
Now asks to have
Existence shorn
The horror of
This life he led
Now begs the mercy
Of the dead
This Apocalypse
Of war-
Does anyone know
What it's for?

29. Mr. Smith Goes To Washington

In Capra's Drama-Comedy
Of Freedom and Morality
James Stewart
Innocent, naive
Gives us a reason
To believe
That values taught
Both good and just
Cannot be bought
Or ground to dust
As Senator,
Stewart's selected
As Mr. Smith
Goes, unelected,
To our capitol
Where he
Can champion
Democracy
He wants to build
A boys camp where
Boys touch the earth
And taste the air
Where Boy Rangers

Can briefly see
How they can live,
What they can be,
But Smith discovers
Power, greed,
Are all men think
They want or need
His ideals mocked,
His world a sham,
They want and do not give
A dam!
Mr. Smith, alone reveals
Upon the Senate floor, ideals,
His courage and
Determination
Rally hope
Throughout the nation
His honest words
Ring good and true
Reminding us what
We should do

30. The Treasure Of
The Sierra Madre

A classic story
Old as greed
Of win and fail,
Of want and need
Where Huston Young
And Huston Old
Combine to tell
This tale of gold
Of three men bound
By greed and lust
Until they found
The precious dust
Also uncovering
Inside
What they can show
What they will hide
They tear the mountains
Soul apart
To find the gold
Within its heart
To satisfy the greed
That burns
But in the end

It all returns
To leave them with
One joke
To measure
Life itself-
The Only Treasure

31. Annie Hall

La-De-Da
And far away
Woody's life is
Here to stay
On the silver screen
Revealing
What he's thinking,
How he's feeling
From his analyst
To you
Woody's life is
There to view
All his lovers,
Now and ex,
Penis envy,
Distant sex,
Troubled wit
And self denial
Mingle in his
Movie style
Every phobia
That's known
Will eventually
Be shown

It's angst and more
(Or is it less?)
I leave it
To
You all
To guess

32. The Godfather, Part II

The good and
The awful news
Goes on
In this saga of
Past and present Don
The youthful Don
And the aging son
Seem to have blended
Into One
As ruthless, soulless,
Power-mad
Michael follows the path
Laid down by Dad
Through his prime
And decline
It was his life to choose
Seems that life made
An offer
He couldn't refuse

33. High Noon

Classic western
Honor, pride
Battle evil,
Fear, inside
Cooper, Kelly
Stand apart
Hand in hand,
And heart to heart
To confront
Their destiny
They'd rather
Fight and die
Then flee
Alone they face
Their killers down
To save their honor
And the town
Both do what's right
And what they must,
Leave badge,
And baggage,
In the dust

34. To Kill A Mockingbird

A sin to kill
The bird who brings
Only pleasure
When it sings
A sin to see
The truth and be
Betrayed by fear's
Dishonesty
Peck, as Atticus,
Reveals
To all, how Truth
And Honor feels
The sleepy South
Both black and white
Where Passions struggle,
Wrong from right,
As Innocent,
And Innocence,
Bigotry and
Common sense
All struggle in this
Atmosphere
Of prejudice
And truth and fear

His children learn
That victory
Is not always
What one can see
As Atticus
Walks, clear of eye,
"Stand up,
Your father's passing by."
He told his children
"Judge when you
Have stood inside
The others shoe"
Their father
Standing brave and tall
Revealed their mockingbirds
To all...

35. It Happened One Night

Screwball comedy
Takes flight
With Gable and Colbert
One night
Unlikely pairing,
Cinderella
In reverse,
Rich lass, poor fella
Snobby heiress feels
She's fated
For a life
Unconsummated
Flees the scene
And ends up liking
Newsman with whom
She's hitchhiking
Spends night together,
Nothing dirty,
Remember it's the
1930's,
Like Jericho,
Sheets separating
Them
Prevents them both

From mating
And protects
Their reputation
In this awkward
Situation
Reluctantly,
Both then discovers
If not star crossed,
They're screw balled,
Lovers
Love triumphs over
Caste and cash-
The Trumpet sounds,
The Walls go
Crash!

36. Midnight Cowboy

Sordid, downbeat, tale of sliding
Down, to where our fears are hiding
Voight and Hoffman illustrate
A slice of life we fear and hate
Homeless drifters in a city,
Offering no hope or pity,
Voight, stud innocent, conspirers
To ignite rich gal's desires
Hoffman's 'Ratso' Rizzo's drive
Is to keep himself alive
This unlikely, sordid sharing
Strangely bonds the pair in caring
For each other, and to see
Dreams become reality
But it ends in Voight just trying
To survive, as 'Ratso's dying,
Racing to a warmer clime,
Voight commits an awful crime
Shining on dreams unfulfilled,
Sunshine shows where hope was killed
Death takes dreams, as well as friend,
Nobody's talkin' at the end,
Closing eyes, as if he's prayin'
He don't hear a word they're sayin'

37. The Best Years
Of Ours Lives

Goldwyn blends
Romance and tears
With comedy in
"The Best Years
Of Our Lives"-
A masterpiece,
Showing men come home,
To peace
Three men returning
Back from war,
Will ask themselves,
"What was it for?"
Fredric March
And Myrna Loy
Share each others
Pain and joy,
Dana Andrews
Finds adjustment
Defines what difficulty
Must meant
Harold Russell
Shows that hearts
Define a man

More than his parts
A 'feel good' and
Heartwarming story
That fills our souls
With love's own glory
A classic drama,
And much more
With H. Carmichael
Keeping score

38. Double Indemnity

Wilder's classic

Film noir thriller

Femme fatal and

Lady Killer

Witty hard-boiled,

Sleazy version

Of two murderers

Perversion

Insurance guy, MacMurray's

Pliant

Toward killing Stanwyck's

Husband-client

Lust and money

Fuel temptation

To create this situation

But we know

From the beginning

This crime's got

No hope of winning

The perfect murder

Gets unraveled

By E. G. Robinson

Whose traveled

Down this road

Lots, and can tell
A claim that's good or bad,
By smell!
The crimes exposed-
It's all for naught
As she gets killed,
And he gets caught
He killed for money,
And the dame,
And saw it all
Go up in flame

39. Doctor Zhivago

In a fugue of huge proportions
Filled with history's distortions
Pasternak and David Lean
Bring soap opera to the screen
The doomed romantic tale they tell,
Is sumptuous, and cold as hell,
Zhivago, as played by Sharif,
A dashing dupe beyond belief,
Spends both the movie, and his life,
Between his lover and his wife
Laura, played by Julie Christie,
(Hear balalaika, see eyes misty)
Is both character and theme
Through every labyrinthine scene
Their throbbing, sobbing, hopeless story
Through snow swept steppes
For love's own glory
Illustrates that great romance
Against the fates ain't got a chance!
Three hours plus we come to find
Zhivago losing girl, and mind,
As Grandeur is, but story's not
And opera triumphs over plot
It's vast and sweeping panorama
Presented in the place of drama

40. North By Northwest

Hitchcock's Classic

Comic Thriller

Is tongue in cheek

And knife in Killer

As Cary Grant,

Eva M. Saint,

Get stuck in

Characters they ain't

North by North West

Is a bearing

That there is

No hope of sharing

And a clue to

Hitchcocks plot

That what appears

To be, is not!

It's murder, mayhem

Flight and spies,

Truth and innocence,

And lies

As twists and turns

Invade this plot

And Grant becomes

A man who's not

In trains and
Under planes he'll flee
Until, the final scene
We'll see
How evil loses
By a nose-
In perfect Hitchcock
Mystery prose!

41. West Side Story

Bard's love story
Re-related
Star crossed lovers
Lives are fated
By their families'
Abhorrence
In New York, this time,
Not Florence,
With Sharks and Jets
And gangs colliding
Bernstein's musical
Is hiding
Truth and pathos
Rights and wrongs-
A fabric wrapped
In dance and songs
Their love burns bright
Though we can see
This is Romantic
Tragedy
We'd hoped that love
Might conquer hate
Alas, we find

That's not their fate
The star crossed lovers
Fall to Earth-
Which gives their story
Lasting worth

42. Rear Window

Hitchcock's Voyeuristic Thriller
Of invalid and lady killer
Finds bored and
Incapacitated
Jimmy Stewart,
Playing sated
Broken picture taker
Viewing
What the other neighbor's doing
As he's spying
From apartment
Grace Kelly's trying
'Cause her heart meant
To ensnare him
In a marriage,
House and home
And baby carriage,
The windows of
Apartment frames,
Like stories all,
Have separate names
Miss Lonely hearts,
Upon the shelf,
Miss Torso and,

Hitchcock, himself,
The Newly Weds,
A song man writing,
Sick wife, salesman,
Yelling, fighting
Like a cast,
Within a play,
As leg in cast
He spends his day
And sees, he thinks,
The salesman's wife
Separated from her life!
He calls the cops
But they can't find
The body that
He has in mind
They finally find
Her resting place
As cops get guy
And he gets Grace

43. King Kong

Mighty Monkey
Little men
Beast and Beauty
Meet again
Expedition
Jungle Style
Captures Kong
For New York Isle
Displayed on stage
Kong runs amok
Goes into rage,
Folks scream and duck
He grabs his love,
And, her in hand,
Kong tramples through
Manhattan land
Now perched atop
The Empire State
Kong roars defiance
At his fate
Fighter planes
Invade the city
Shoot Kong and change
Our fear to pity

One final look,
Kong falls to meet
His death upon
The New York street
But love, not bullets,
Were released,
For it was
'Beauty killed the Beast!'

44. The Birth Of A Nation

The most important film
You'll see,
This biased view
Of history
Astonishing,
Repulsive lies
A masterpiece
Of film that tries
To use the cinema
As art
And show how war
Tears lives apart
Griffith portrays
KKK
As Southern Knights
Who save the day
It's movie
Documentary
Rewriting
Southern history
And helps perpetuate
Their fate
Of a hundred years
Of hate

As war and peace
And Reconstruction
Help to seal
The South's destruction
With every
Cinematic trick
Used to make
His lessons stick,
It's history
Writ up
By lightning
Controversial
Brilliant,
Frightening!

45. A Streetcar Named Desire

Hot New Orleans
World on fire
Life and streetcar
Named Desire
From the pen
Of Tennessee
Flows brutal
Eccentricity
Into this world
With passions name
Drifts Blanch Du Bois
Consumed with shame
Sister Stella
Takes her in
To a world of
Pain and sin
No strangers kindness
Finds she near,
Instead a world
Of primal fear
Brando's Kowalski
Takes his lust
And grinds her sanity
To dust

But find at last
That his desires
Consumes their lives
In savage fires
Left alone
He cries her name-
"Stella"
Leaves him
Just his shame

46. A Clockwork Orange

Kubrick's film
From Burgess's pages
Burns with
Nihilistic rages
A future where
All sanity
Bereft of its
Humanity
As ultra-violence
Sets the stage
For fights and nights
Of wild rampage
Where law and order
Both have fled
Leaving horror
In its stead
Rape and pillage
Have their days
Till cops nab Alex
Now who pays
For his life of
Mad destruction
By cerebral
Reconstruction

A clockwork orange
Becomes his fate
Everything he loved-
He'll hate
Evil and free will
Bereft
Inside his soul
There's nothing left
No wrong, no right
He has no voice,
A creature without
Moral choice
But by 'curing' him,
The State
Has now become
The Thing they hate
And so to be
What they extol
They must return
His Evil Soul!

47. Taxi Driver

Scorsese, Schrader
And DeNero
Gritty, film noir
Anti hero
Lonely, obsessed,
Alienated,
Angry at a world
He hated
New York as an
Allegory,
Existential,
Hell's own story
Taxi driver,
Anger filling
His existence,
Plans on killing
All the human scum
That clutter,
And surround him,
In the gutter
Schizophrenic,
Paranoid,
Delusional and,
Self destroyed,

To clean the city

He is willing

To engage in

Bloody killing

As gun and foreplay

Get confused

It's hard to tell

Which one is used

He finally rescues

Jody Foster

Returns her to

The home

That lost her

Becomes a hero,

His delusion,

Is complete

At film's conclusion

48. Jaws

People laughing
Happy scene
Peaceful beach
With sea serene
While underneath
Its crashing depth,
Waits a thrashing,
Slashing death
Swimmer cries out,
Disappears,
Leaves behind
A wake of fears
Great White has
Invaded Amity
Holiday becomes
Calamity!
City fathers
Need to clear
Waters of this
Floating fear
Offer bounty,
Just can't wait
Old salt,
Name of Quint,

Takes bait

Sails his boat

To orca-slay,

Plus settle scores

And save the day,

He finds the fish

Fish bites the boat

And swallows Quint

But while afloat

Is blown apart

By single shot

Some days you're lucky

Others not!

A classic tale

Of Fish and Men-

And just when you thought it was safe

to go into the waters again.......

49. Snow White And The Seven Dwarfs

Disney's moving art is seen
Glowing on the silver screen
Classic Evil Witch hates beauty
Needs to be the realms top cutie
Magic mirror sets her right
"Fairest in the land?" Not quite!
Witch wants White to wind up dead
White winds up with dwarfs instead
Stock of characters includes
Seven dwarfs, aka-Moods:
Doc and Dopey, Bashful, Happy
Short and looking sort of sappy
Also Sneezy, Sleepy, Grumpy
Ditto on the short and lumpy
All pledge to protect the maid
From the evil plans Witch made
Too late! White bites apple red
Winds up looking dead, instead
Dwarfs have White in beauty lay
In a crystal like display
Handsome prince sees,
Gives a kiss,
Awakens White from Death's abyss
Happy Ever After Day-
Of course it had to end this way

50. Butch Cassidy And The Sundance Kid

Last of the Wild West

Bandit Breed

Butch and Sundance

Find they need

Banks or rail cars

They can rob

Or else they'll have

To get a job!

The 1900's

Pinkerton

Boys have got them

On the run

(Though witty, sly and

Long on looks,

Butch and Sundance

Both are crooks)

To escape both law

And order

They're forced to flee

South of the border

Bolivia don't change

Their ways

Romantic shootout

Ends their days
These characters
Gave all they had
Transforming good guys
Out of bad

51. The Philadelphia Story

Screwball comedy

Relating

Hepburn, cool,

Sophisticating

Cary Grant who's

Paired and pitted

In a world where

Love's outwitted

Breaking marriage,

And his putter,

Hepburn throws them

Both in gutter

Irreverent

In style and tone

Cukor shows how

Love alone

Can win the war

Of injured masses

Even with

The privileged classes

Stewart has a

Newsman's duty

To interview the

Snooty, beauty

Cast at wedding
Has meandering
Husband, first one,
Plus philandering
Father, mother,
All agreeing
There's no passion
Here worth seeing
Suddenly, we find
Three fires
Trying to warm
Her desires
Groom drops out,
She marries old one,
Asks to have for
Best man, bold one,
Film finale
Shows her vanity
Is no match for
Loves humanity

52. From Here To Eternity

Take a trip
Across the sea
From here, go to
Eternity-
A powerful,
Romantic story
Filled with violence,
And glory
Where war's preamble
Is the lives
Of enlisted men,
And wives,
With prostitutes
And misbegotten
Outcasts, who are
Soon forgotten
Churned together
On the shore
As the world
Burned into war
Lancaster, Debra Kerr,
Both reach
Sandy passions,
On the beach,

Sinatra, playing,
Hard and rough,
Shows Borgnine that
He's got 'the stuff'
The whole ensemble,
Clift and Reed,
Reveal to us,
The truths we need
All casualties
Of Love and War
That question what
They're fighting for
It's military history
Combined with
Passions mystery
That makes us
Realize that we
Are moments in
Eternity

53. Amadeus

Ancient Soliere tells
His life's a symphony
Of Hells
Bested by a bitter fate
That found his talent
Second rate
The gift of the
Eternal Muse
Was never given
Him to use
Amadeus,
Curse his name!
Had his gift,
But like a game
Spent his life,
All never asking
As if the gift were
Everlasting
Now Soliere,
Bitter man,
Curses life,
And God and man
While Mozart's music
Still astounds

Our world with its
Immortal sounds
And Soliere?
Most forgotten-
Sometimes life gets
Pretty rotten

54. All Quiet On The Western Front

For the Fatherland

And glory

On to battle!

Ageless story

While the old

Stay home and save

Life and liberty,

And such

Men lay dying

In their grave

Battle's fodder,

If that much

From their mud and

Trenches tell

There's no glory-

War is always

Hell's own story

55. The Sound Of Music

The hills have never
Seen the likes
As parents, Von Trapp
And their tykes
Flee through fields
Of flowers gay
As they wend their
Merry way
From that nasty
Hitler's Reich
Which they're sure
They wouldn't like
Julie Andrews,
In reprise,
As Deutschland's Poppins
Lights the skies
To fill the
Panoramic screen
With a sweetness
Rarely seen
A picture perfect
Music treat
For those who like
Their strudel sweet

56. M*A*S*H

Altman in his
Movie M*A*S*H
Comments on
Wars' culture clash
Hawkeye, Trapper John
Are seen,
As Hot Lips, Burns
On Radar's screen
Showing suicide
As painless,
Which makes their battles
More than brainless-
Oddball, Ensemble
Comedy
Illustrating, perfectly,
That to maintain
Humanity
You can't retain
Your sanity

57. The Third Man

Graham Green's post war
Film noir thriller
Has the victim as the killer!
Here innocence, naivete'
Are torn apart or swept away
We feel the melancholy theme
Both in the score and on the screen
As Vienna, broken, battered
Throws away those things that mattered
Where good and evil are confused
And everyone is bought or used
Holly Martins (Joseph Cotton)
Visits Harry Lime, who gotten
Killed, or murdered? He knows not-
Which is the essence of the plot-
Lime, as played by Wells', a thug
Who made his money selling drugs
Ana, who both are adoring,
Has survived by classy whoring
Oblique angles and distortions
Symbolize the plots contortions
Bizarre, tilted scenes reveal
Both world and city as surreal
In a dark street, Orson Wells,

97

Has an entrance, non nonpareils,

To show Cotton he's alive

Faking his death to survive

While Cotton knows his old friend sold

Honor, friends and love for gold

Beneath the battered streets, finds Lime

Finally running out of time

While Ana, saved by Holly/Cotton,

Loves the dead Wells, who was rotten,

Cotton did the thing that mattered

Love and innocence lie shattered

Existential tale of losing

And the cost of what we're choosing...

58. Fantasia

Art and Music here combined
Illuminating screen and mind
In a flight across the skies
Of our hearts and ears and eyes
Bach's fugues, Tchaikovsky's music prance
Across the screen in floral dance
As fairies, cossacks, seasons all
Show Summer, Winter, Spring and Fall
The sorcerers apprentice tells
Of Mouse and music, magic spells,
Combined to have enchantment bring
A prologue to The Rite Of Spring
From Earth's creation, Life's travails
Stravinsky's music weaves its tales
Through birth, through death and in between
Life's cataclysm's heard and seen
And, for a moment now, a bow,
A word,
To Soundtrack, or no sound be heard!
Beethoven's muse and soul serene
In Pastoral symphonic scene
Have gods and goddesses cavort
Across Elysian fields in sport
While Bacchus, cupids, centaurs play

Till Zeus' lightning ends their day

Apollo's chariot makes its run

To mark the setting of the sun

And dusky twilight covers all

As Morpheus' cloak lets darkness fall

Wake up!

It's time to see The Dance

Of Hours, as ostrich, hippo prance

The Great Hall shows us all today

Alligator, elephant ballet!

All pirouette, and leap for you

In huge and dainty pa de deux

Corps de ballet like none you've seen

At once bizarre yet most serene

Fantasia ends with death and light

Celebrating day and night

Bald Mount, Ave' Marie conclude

This visual, musical, interlude

A feast for eyes and ears and hearts

A Sum much greater than its parts

59. Rebel Without A Cause

James Dean, in life
And role, combined
Indelibly,
Upon our mind,
The image of
The Rebel tall
We felt was living
In us all
The heart that
No one understood
The bad that struggled
With the good
His real and
Reel life both
Were racing
Down life's road
Where fate was pacing-
Then time ran out
And nothing mattered
Life and hopes
And dreams

Lay shattered
Leaving memories
To spin
Of how we lost
What might have been

60. Raiders Of The Lost Ark

Take every serial
You've seen-
Put all the best parts
On the screen
Get an adventure
New and old
With evil villains,
Heroes bold
Both racing on a
Long lost quest
The Treasured Ark!
You'll get the best
Adventure filled with
Skulls and bones
Escapes, and treasures-
Indy Jones
Fedora, bullwhip,
Look of ease,
'Obtainer of
Antiquities'
Ford and Spielberg
Spin a story,
That's Adventure-
Allegory

Good and Evil,
Light and Dark-
All searching for
An Ancient Ark
There's fights, entombments,
Rescues, forces,
Chases on trucks,
Airplanes, horses,
Plus other great
Adventure scenes
As action overflows
The screens
In the end,
Bad melts away
As good, that's Indy,
Saves the day
Plus Ark and lady,
Honor, glory,
But that, of course,
Another story

61. Vertigo

Hitchcock's movie
Mesmerizes
Jimmy Stewart
Realizes
In this psyco-
Suspense-thriller
That acrophobia's
A killer!
Cop, retired,
Tries to be
At peace with
Disability
As Scottie, Stewart
Is obsessed
As Madeline,
Novak's possessed
Following her,
Stewart meets
A vortex of
His past repeats
As love and terror
Are combined
With lies and truth
To fool our mind

He sees, he thinks,

Her suiciding

Real, or murder

Someone's hiding?

She's uncovered

In confusion,

He discovers death's

Illusion

Nothing he believed

Had mattered

Reality and truth

Lie shattered

He confronted

Love and fear

And, in the end,

Both disappear

62. Tootsie

Dustin Hoffman,
Keeps them guessing,
For employment,
He's cross dressing
Unemployed,
He's forced to fake
The distaff role
And undertake
To have his
Feminine side rule
His acting life
So he can fool-
Tootsie's clearly
Demonstrating,
Often
What we love,
We're hating
And, sometimes
We have to feel
Phoney,
To find out what's real
Dustin's actions
Start revealing
Feelings he was

Scared of feeling
Sometimes to be
A woman can
Make one be
A better man

63. Stagecoach

John Ford's film
Reality
Presents a play,
Morality,
In a classic
Western way
Where good and evil
Have their day
And social issues,
Major themes,
Are intertwined
With hopes and dreams
Here gallantry,
Nobility,
Compete with false
Civility
Where those who claim
To be the best
All fail to pass
The moral test
John Wayne, Kid Ringo,
Shootist bold,
Loves fallen Dallas,
Heart of gold,

And seems to, with
A single hand,
Protect them from
The Indian band,
Do justice, get respect,
All while
He resurrects
Film, western style
Where good and bad
Morality
Are shown in their
Totality
And evil men will
Always meet
Their fate upon
Some dusty street
The genre's never
Had to change
Since 'Duke' Wayne rode
The purple range

64. Close Encounters
Of The Third Kind

Spielberg has us
Turn our eyes
To watch the dark
Enchanted skies
For Close Encounters
From afar
For creatures from
Another star
A dazzling treat
Of sound and light
Illuminating
Day and night
To illustrate
What we have known
Within our hearts-
We're not alone!
These Close Encounters
Show a part
Of what lies hidden
In our heart
Combining our reality
With other world's
Totality

Where beings from
Another place
Can move through seas
Of Time and Space
In structures built
Of sound and light
They reach to touch us
In the night,
Like children from
A distant land
Man reaches out
To touch their hand

65. The Silence Of The Lambs

Anthony Hopkins
Is a winner,
As Hannibal Lector
Serves you dinner
It's quid pro quo
For Agent Starling,
As psycho-killer,
FBI darling,
Swap insights,
And information,
On a grisly
Situation
Each invades
The others mind
As pain pervades
Their search to find
The truth behind
Those words that lie
Behind the dark
Unflinching eye
As Innocence
She's consummating
Lector,
Evil, incarnating

To catch the killer,

And to find,

The dark recesses

Of his mind

As teacher, father,

Pupil, guide

Both feel, reveal,

Those things they hide

The Silence Of

The Lambs reveal

Thrills' Horror we're

Afraid to feel

And leaves us with

This Special treat:

You really are

Just who you eat!

66. Network

Anchorman begins to tell
All the world,
He's Mad as Hell
Wants to even up the score
He won't take it
Anymore!
Video execs tear hair
Want to take him
Off the air
On the electronic stage
Howard's rage is
All the rage
Informs his audience
That he
Will blow his brains out
On TV
Yet in the end,
Execs instead
Have their assassins
Shoot him dead
Was the cause
The public hatings?
Or was he killed
For lousy ratings?

67. The Manchurian Candidate

A film, suppressed

For thirty years,

Where nothing is

As first appears

Laurence Harvey's mind

Is fated

As an instrument

Created

To obey a

Dark command

Written by a

Foreign hand

Sinatra questions,

Quite psychotic,

From suggestions,

Post hypnotic

A. Lansbury

Taking parts

Is evil mother,

Queen of hearts,

Hallucinary mystery,

Too close to

Recent history,

Cynical, sophisticated,

Disturbing plot
You loved or hated
Shocking,
Mesmerizing part-
A legendary work of art

68. An American In Paris

With music bursting
At its seams
In a Paris
Of our dreams,
Kelly and Caron
Romance
Their lives away
In song and dance
Gershwin's music's
Synchronizing
Kelly, as he's
Rhapsodizing
Caron with his
Flying feet
In this Technicolor treat
First he wins her,
Then he loses,
Throws reality aside
And chooses
To pursue in fantasy
The love lost in reality
A classic ballet
Through the pages
Of great

Impressionistic sages,
Has Kelly and Caron
Revealing
The love they know
They both are feeling
Though 'Singing in the Rain'
It ain't,
Dancing through
This World of Paint,
Their love, it's clear,
Is here to stay-
Who'd have it
Any other way?

69. Shane

Timeless classic
Allegory
Good and evil
Western story
Alan Ladd,
As Shane's
Terrific
Pearl handled,
Clad in buckskin-
Mythic!
No place for him
His time has past
But fate intrudes,
The die is cast
For one last time,
The dusty street
Where good and evil
Come to meet
Although he tried
It couldn't last
His present's
Fated to his past
Victorious,
He bids goodbye

As Joey, sadly,
Starts to cry,
He leaves returning
Where he came-
The mountains echo back
His name...

70. The French Connection

Hackman's "Popeye",

Cop sadistic-

Vulgar, brutal,

Realistic!

Gritty city,

Cop pursuing

Suave Frenchman

He knows is doing

Big time score

Of hot narcotic

Driving "Popeye"

More psychotic

His compulsion

To arrest him

Is a passion

That obsessed him

Pursuing Frog he

Feels he can

Break the laws

Of God or man

Down streets, in bars,

The Frog he's chasing

Under elevated trains-

He's racing!

In the end,
It's all disaster
A fickle fate proves
It is master
As Frog gets free
Cops life is lost
Was any of this
Worth the cost?

71. Forrest Gump

Every single
Great Event
Seemed to be seen
By this Humble Gent
Not only seen,
But in that minute
Gump inserted himself
Right in it!
Although his life was
'Bid, no trump'
You can't see the Forrest
For the Gump!

72. Ben-Hur

Old Judea
Bible flicks
Jew and Roman,
Tight as ticks
One mistake,
And Ben-Hur gains
A life of slavery
In chains
Mom and sister
Thrown in cell—
Very close to
Living Hell—
Ben redeems
His life and saves
Roman, self, from
Ocean graves
(Confronts Messala,
Former friend,
Says, 'Free my kin
Or life will end!')
Revenge will have
Its proper place
In bold,
No holds barred,

Chariot race
The Roman's black
The Jew is white,
No problems choosing
Wrong from right,
Ben's tough, but pure,
Messala's lust,
Ben finds him,
Grinds him
In the dust
A fabled tale,
Of virtues past
Plus one Commandment:
Get him last!

73. Wuthering Heights

Bronte's Masterpiece
Is told
As passion and revenge
Enfold
A classic drama
Of romance
Where happy endings
Have no chance
Oberon, Olivier
As Cathy, Heathcliff,
Laugh and play
As child companions,
Who, soulmated,
Destiny and love
Has fated
Upon the moors
Their timeless story
Of Love's
Everlasting Glory
Shows they can't be
Separated
From a destiny

That's fated:
Pursuing Love
With Single Breath-
More powerful
Than time or death

74. The Gold Rush

The pantomime of life
Is told
With Chaplin's tramp
In search of gold
As Chaplin weaves
His style unique
In Comic Drama
Pathetique
As miners brave
The Northern cold
Searching for
Alaskan gold
Tramp eats his boot
To stay alive-
It's foot in mouth
So they'll survive
Now, bootlessly, he
Gets the chance
With Georgia, showgirl
For a dance
He falls in love,
And falls to floor,
And wants to marry
His amour

The Tramp helps lost
Big Jim to find
The gold mine that
Had slipped his mind
Now rich, he finds
The Miss he's missing
As movie ends,
We see them kissing

75. Dances With Wolves

Costner,
Actor and Director
Takes a monumental
Vector
To a sentimental
Story
That's best western
Allegory
Where he strips
His white veneer
So that he
Can see and hear
The frontier as
It's meant to be
Before becoming
History
In the Endless West's
Last places
As its solitude,
Embraces
Costner
We can see him find
Wolves that dance
Within his mind

In him feel
The wind and rain,
The bison's thunder
On the plain
The Sioux, whose wisdom
Helps him see
This Land's Eternal
Harmony
Rarely has
The West been seen
So lovingly
Upon the screen
With clarity
We see the cost
Of how the West
Was won,
And lost...

76. City Lights

The Quintessential Chaplin's
Seen
Silently,
Upon the screen
As comic romance
Pantomime
Undimmed by sound,
Or space or time
Before, he bids
A fond 'Adieu'
The Tramp reveals
Life's Truths to you
How goodness,
And the very kind,
Are clearly seen
Though one is blind
Every comic art routine
The Little Tramp
Brings to the screen
Shows how the heart
And soul reveal
More than words
What people feel
And, in the end,

We see the light
As the blind girl
Gets her sight
She's seen the kind
And gentle soul
Of the Tramp
Who made her whole
Loves face smiles back,
What can we say?
They just stopped
Making them
This way

77. American Graffiti

American as anything
Lucas makes the 60's sing
In a single night appears
Teenage tales
Of hopes and fears
As Wolfman's music
Stokes their fires
Defining passions
And desires-
See Ron Howard (Steve)
Whose leaving
Cindy Williams (Laurie)
Grieving,
Dick Dreyfuss (as Curt)
Sees conclusive
Love, as gorgeous, blond,
Elusive,
Suzanne Summers
In a white
Thunderbird
Floats through the night
Harrison Ford's (Falfa)
Races
One of many

Actors faces
Now grown older
Lets us know
This time was really
Long ago!

78. Rocky

He's the Long Shot
Tough and mean
Out to grab
His Crazy Dream
Against all odds
He does his thing
And finds his place
Inside the ring
Bloody, broken,
Still unbowed,
He wins the fight,
The girl, the crowd!
But who knew when
He first begun
That this would just be
Rocky I?

79. The Deer Hunter

One Clear Shot,
Without a doubt,
Is what this movie's
All about
Roulette as deadly
Metaphor
For the craziness
Of war
Shows how some live,
Others die,
With no one knowing
Who or why
With the war's
Disintegrating
Entity of death
And hating,
We see how lives
Are torn asunder
Under battles'
Ruthless thunder
A macho parable
Of death
That makes the viewer

Hold their breath
And hold the horrors
Deep inside
Leaving not
One place to hide

80. The Wild Bunch

The world had changed
But these guys wouldn't
The Earth had cooled
But these guys couldn't
A last adventure
One more shooting
All they wanted
Was more looting!
Revolution
South of border
Seemed a project
Made to order
Guns erupting
Bullets flying
Gore and glory
People dying
In the end
The past is served
What they wanted
And deserved:
Blaze of Glory-
End of story!

81. Modern Times

With derby hat
And baggy pants
Chaplin gave us
One last chance
To prepare,
In pantomimes,
The brand new world
Of Modern Times
The industries
Have made him slog
Through work as if
He were a cog
The Tramp,
As Everyman, is seen
Just as a part
Of the Machine
With soul and body
Ground at work
His spirit snaps-
He goes berserk!
Tossed out, alone,
He finally meets
Paulette Goddard
On the streets

Through misadventures
Thick and thin
The Tramp is sure
That Love will win
He know that life's
A lovely song
"Buck up",
He says, "We'll get along!"
Some times are modern,
Some are past,
Through all of them
True love will last
The Little Tramp
Helps us to see
Inside our hearts
We're always free!

82. Giant

Stevenson's
Defining great
Saga of the
Lone Star State
Pits the world
Of Texas Old
Against the world
Of Texas Bold
Rock Hudson, rancher,
Stolid, stoic,
Bigoted,
At times heroic,
Verses James Dean
Sullen, mythic
And, in his final role,
Terrific
Ethereal,
Liz Taylor sees,
And understands,
Their destinies
As oil and cattle
Wage a fight
Where no one's wrong
And no one's right

In the end,

We see the changes

Within the hearts,

And on the ranges,

As Texas Old

Lets go its past

So Texas New

Can live at last

It's good old, down home

Barbeque

A Giant, Texas treat

Come true!

83. Platoon

Oliver Stone
Tells war's story
Honest, brutal,
Stripped of glory,
Men who come
Filled up with hope
And leave filled up
With death and dope
Charlie Sheen, as Chris,
Narrating
On the death and fear
And hating
In the mud and crud
They're willing
To engage in
Wanton killing
Of the foe or,
Of each other-
Kill your enemy,
Or brother
Burn the village,
Kill your friend,
Death continues
Without end

Here see war's
Reality
Stripped of all
Morality
Young men who
In spite of trying
To survive,
End up by dying
Or survive
In mindless hell
For a cause
No one can tell
Stones film shows
The immensity
Of wars
Insane Intensity

84. Fargo

A swirling storm
A swirling life
A contract made
Upon a wife
The most inept
Of crooks around
Are set to stumble
Into town
They first commit
A grisly crime
Police Chief,
Pregnant at the time,
Investigates but,
All too late,
The ransomed wife
Has met her fate
From this point on
It's all bad fun
With people killed,
Or on the run,
Bad guys, both sides,
Out of time
Cold day, no pay,

For this days crime

P.G. Chief

Gets case resolved

As she delivers-

Case is solved

85. Duck Soup

The Brothers Marx
Once more
Explore,
Absurdities
Of class and war
In a genre
Where they bump
Bombastic stuffed shirts
On the rump
Lunacy, wit,
And satire,
Are used as weapons
To conspire
Against, no sense
Pomposities,
Of wars immense
Monstrosities
Any similarity
To plot,
In this hilarity
Is not
Rather, absurdality
In place of
Hard reality

Illustrates
Far more than fact
How foolishly
We look and act
A film to savor
And to save-
"Hail Freedonia,
Land of the brave..."

86. Mutiny On The Bounty

A Nautical
Adventure treat
As on the Bounty's decks
We met
Good and evil
Eye to eye-
Fletcher Christian,
Captain Bligh
Bligh, as played by
Charles Laughton,
Is tyrannical,
And rotten,
Christian, first mate,
Played by Gable
Does the only thing
He's able
Protecting crew
From cruelty
He declares
A mutiny!
As Bligh gets put
Into a boat,
Barely big enough
To float,

Christian and his men
Go find
The paradise
They left behind
Bligh, amazingly, survives,
Returns to take
His old crew's lives
But, in court,
They win, he lost
Each got their life,
And paid their cost...

87. Frankenstein

Doctor Frankenstein's
Dissecting
Tons of corpses
And selecting
An organ here,
A muscle there
A piece of bone
A hank of hair
Pretty soon he
Has collected
All the parts
Which are connected
In a man like form
Together
(Outside lightning,
Stormy weather)
Doc in laboratory
Creeping
While, below,
The town lies sleeping
Throws the switch
The monster's waken
Doctor and assistant
Shaken

Bursting bonds

Docs new creation

Yearns to test

His animation

Roams the countryside

And finds

People scared out

Of their minds

World's not ready,

Pays the toll,

Mighty body,

Simple soul,

We do the very

Best we can-

Who's the monster?

Who's the man?

88. Easy Rider

Peter Fonda,

Henrys son,

On his Harley

Makes a run

Through our country,

Here to there,

But couldn't find it

Anywhere

Nights and days

He views the nation

Through his dazed

Hallucination

In the end,

He finds his road

Where the river

Waters flowed

Only wanted

To be free

The way it all

Turned out to be

89. Patton

George C. Scott
Salutes unseen
Troops upon
The silver screen
Exhorting them
To fight and try
"To make those
Nazi bastards die!"
In other words
To now become
As bad as they are,
And then some!
Standing proud-
Red, white and blue
Saluting both
Himself, and you,
His look, both cold
And mean, tells all,
An Ego, waiting
For The Fall...

90. The Jazz Singer

Jolson spreads his arms
And brings
Sound and music
When he sings
The movies' voices
Have been found
As Jolson's 'Mammy'
Gives it sound
Torn between
Two worlds, he has
To choose between
His faith and jazz
On opening night
A painful choice-
Perform or give
'Kol Nidre' voice
He gets both
Obligations met
Then says,
"You ain't heard
Nothin' yet"
Technology
And art combined
To weave this movie

In our mind
Al Jolson, with
His arms unfurled
Embraces 'Mammy,'
And the world

91. My Fair Lady

The rain falls sweetly
On the plain
Cockney, Doolittle,
By name,
A flower girl,
Prof. Higgins knows
He can transform
From head to toes
Into a lady
Filled with graces
Befitting those
Born in high places
Rex Harrison's
Sophisticated
Audrey Hepburn's
Captivated
(Stanley Holloway's
Soon mated)
Without a kiss,
Or touch, they'll find
A 'proper love'
Is on their mind
Shaw's 'Pygmalion'
Is seen,

Joyously,
Upon the screen
Lowe and Learner's
Songs take flight
And make you want
To dance all night

92. A Place In The Sun

Dreiser's tale
Of love and hate
And how our lives
Are ruled by fate
Or in an instant,
Cease to be,
Are shown as
American Tragedy
Stevens film noir
Darkly chooses
How both rich
And poor confuses
Love, ambition,
And desires,
In the heat of
Passion's fires
Taylor, Clift,
And Winters toying
With each others lives,
Destroying,
Everything
They hoped would be,
Ending up
In tragedy!

93. The Apartment

Lemmon, MacLaine

In apartment

Try to tell us

What their hearts meant

She's involved with

Boss, philandering,

Who promised

Wedding band or ring

Womanizing boss,

MacMurray,

Isn't in much

Of a hurry

She discovers

He's a pack of lies

"That's the way it

Crumbles, cookie-wise,"

Lemmon says,

His love is real

Says she, "OK,

Shut up and deal!"

It's comedy, served

Bittersweet,

Where, sometimes,

Even love can meet

94. Goodfellas

Scorsese's art
Presents a time,
A place, a world,
A life of crime-
A document
We won't forget
Of bad times that
We don't regret
No finer film
Has yet been seen
Of Mafioso's
On the screen
Of dons
And killers,
Husbands, wives
Of wrong decisions,
Wasted lives
And how the values
That they swear
Allegiance to
Without a care
May later have them
Forced to try
To let part of

Their honor die
The guilt they feel
Is not the sin,
But that they want it
Back again!

95. Pulp Fiction

Tarantino

Spins a story

Lurid, elegant and gory

Where three plots are

Intertwined

To amuse, confuse

Your mind

Here Jackson spouts

The Scriptures, killing

With Travolta,

Who is willing,

To date Thurman,

Bosses wife,

Dances, she O. D.'s,

Saves life-

Willis, boxer,

Won't throw fight,

Converted Jackson

Sees the light

Twists and turns

In plot dramatic

Weave confusing,

Enigmatic

Tale that at the end

Is bending

End to front

At final ending-

As a character

Expected

To be dead is

Resurrected

So, somehow,

This most confusing

Violence gets

Quite amusing

Moral, visceral, profane

A plot

By any other name...

96. The Searchers

What makes a man to wander?
What makes a man to roam?
What makes a man leave bed and board
And turn his back on home?*

In our greatest western story
John Ford tells, in allegory,
Of a man, come back to find
A soul, a life he left behind
John Wayne, as Ethan, stands apart,
He's closed his mind and locked his heart
And seen his brothers family,
Which could have been his destiny,
Destroyed by Indians who ravage,
Rape and slaughter, with a savage
Heart that beats to primal drums-
Now, savage as they, he becomes
Tracking them through miles and years
Ethan must confront his fears
He finds revenge, is like a knife,
Savaging the heart of life
Isolated, he is fated
To protect what he has hated
Now, standing in the swirling dust,

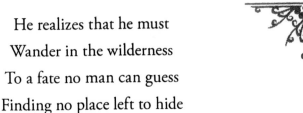

He realizes that he must
Wander in the wilderness
To a fate no man can guess
Finding no place left to hide
In either world, he's left outside...
Man searches everywhere to find
In heart and soul some peace of mind

*But where, Oh Lord, Oh where?

97. Bringing Up Baby

Screwball comedy,
Relating
Absurd and
Humiliating
Characters pushed
To extremes
Through coincidental scenes
Cary Grant
And Hepburn's Baby
Is a leopard
Who just may be
Cupid's arrow's
Furry feather
Bringing both of them
Together
Hepburn's opposite
Of humbling
Grant's bespectacled,
And bumbling,
Scientist,
Eccentric heiress,
Show us what a
Zany pair is
As a dinosaur bone's

Cast

As a buried,

Dogs repast,

In a plot where

Misadventures

Almost make us

Lose our dentures

Laughing at their

Breathless pace

Plot lines somehow

Fall in place

To keep this 'Baby'

On the run

As Ruthlessly

Romantic

Fun!

98. Unforgiven

Eastwoods character
Is driven
Bitter, hard and
Unforgiven
To redeem himself
He must
Trample all his
Life to dust
One last time
Now it's his fate
To become
The man he'll hate
He does his job
And leaves to live
Hoping others
Will forgive
He finds they do
Yet knows that he
Cannot forgive
His destiny

99. Guess Who's Coming To Dinner

Tracy, Hepburn

Have to dinner

Daughter's fiancé

Plus inner

Soul/heart searching

Introspection

Regarding

Son in law selection

Corny, truthful,

But revealing

What our inner

Selves are feeling

In the end

They do what's right

And find out life's

Not black and white!

100. Yankee Doodle Dandy

Cagney's George M. Cohan's
Seen,
Red, white and blue
Upon the screen
A patriotic dancing fest
Overflowing with the best
Of songs and dance
In celebration
Of Our Grand Old Flag,
And nation,
It's Yankee Doodle,
Over There,
July the fourth,
Without a care
Our country's colors,
Pure and bright,
All brought to you
In black and white!

CPSIA information can be obtained
at www.ICGtesting.com
Printed in the USA
FSOW01n1551170615
8041FS